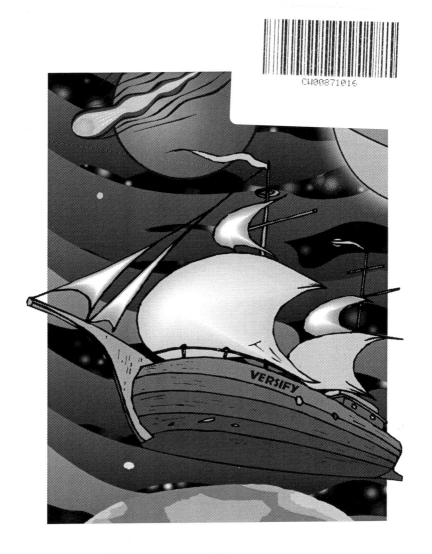

POETIC VOYAGES
CARMARTHENSHIRE

Edited by Dave Thomas

First published in Great Britain in 2001 by
YOUNG WRITERS
Remus House,
Coltsfoot Drive,
Peterborough, PE2 9JX
Telephone (01733) 890066

HB ISBN 0 75433 092 3
SB ISBN 0 75433 093 1

FOREWORD

Young Writers was established in 1991 with the aim to promote creative writing in children, to make reading and writing poetry fun.

This year once again, proved to be a tremendous success with over 88,000 entries received nationwide.

The Poetic Voyages competition has shown us the high standard of work and effort that children are capable of today. It is a reflection of the teaching skills in schools, the enthusiasm and creativity they have injected into their pupils shines clearly within this anthology.

The task of selecting poems was therefore a difficult one but nevertheless, an enjoyable experience. We hope you are as pleased with the final selection in *Poetic Voyages Carmarthenshire* as we are.

CONTENTS

Llanybydder Primary School

Rhodri Evans	64
Oliver Florence	65
Paul Bashford	66
Lowri Haf Davies	67
Shaun Ablett	68
Jonathan Davies	69
Jade Jones	70
Alison Lucas	71
David Anthony Jones	72

Llechryd School

Gareth Jones	73
Kelly Morrisey	74
Rebecca Sommerville	75
Wyn Jones	76
Francis Barrett	77
Hannah Curran	78
Antoni Castaglioni	79
Kerry Thomas	80
Aled James	81
John Williams	82
Adrian Hutton	83
Ruth Sommerville	84
Bethan Curran	85
Angharad Rees	86
Megan Williams	87

Nant-Y-Groes Primary School

Kayley Gebbie	88
Anna Davies	89
Leanne Jones	90

Old Road Primary School

Samantha Griffiths	91
Lloyd Davies	92

Joshua Naylor	93
Peter Harris	94
Rebecca Wilkins	95
Timothy Taylor	96
Hayley Evans	97
Kate Davies	98
Rebecca Crabb	99
Sophia Williams	100
Jamie Mends	101
Carolyn Gemma Rees	102
Simon Lewis	103
Michelle Crabb	104
Lorna Gravelle	106
Charlotte Rose Williams	107
Jamie Baier	108
James Southam	109
Ffion Richards	110
Daniel Mark Griffiths	111
Chris Williams	112
Stephen Lott	113
Simon Walters	114
James Lloyd	115
Kimry Coleman	116
Alex Wilkins	117
Andrew Jackson	118
Shaun Caton	119
Daniel James	120

Swiss Valley Primary School

Laura Thomas	121
Sally Davies	122
Nikita Poli	123
Lauren Sourbutts	124
Hannah Morris	125
Arianwen Caiach-Taylor	126

Ysgol Gynradd Cwmgors

The Poems

THE GRIZZLY BEAR

I have a little grizzly bear,
His fur is golden brown,
He climbs the mountains
He climbs the trees
He swims the lakes and the rivers
And even the deep blue seas.

Gemma Evans (10)
Bigyn CP School

SPACE TOURIST

Three, two, one, blast-off.
The rocket left the Earth.
The tourist in designer spacesuit
Thought what moon dust would be worth.
Perhaps he'd buy a postcard of a crater
Followed by a photo with an alien later.
As he bravely left the shuttle
For the advertised space walk.
As he hurtled through the blackness
The galaxy sped by.
With stars and distant planets
Lighting up the sky.
Mars, Mercury, Neptune, Jupiter,
The tourist thought he saw all four.
Such good value for a bargain-buy space tour.

David Watkins (8)
Bigyn CP School

SPRING

The lambs are out
scurrying about.
The horses neigh
and eat their hay.
The blossoms bloom
not fall in gloom.
The twinkling stars
come out at night.
They light the sky
with a twinkling light.
The daisies start to grow
grow and grow.
Shoots come up
through the snow.

Lowri Betrys Evans (8)
Bigyn CP School

SCHOOL IS COOL

I like school because it's cool
And it's next to a pool.
In school my best mate is Kate
And in the mornings I meet her at the school gate
And we're never ever late!

My teacher's name is Mr Rees
And he's making sure he's got peace.
We try hard in school
And follow every rule.
There's always someone who's a class fool
But I think there is one in every school.

In my school we have lots of cooks
And all of them use cookery books.
Food in my school is really nice
My favourite is curry and rice.
We all like playtime because it's fun
We run around and fall on our bum.

At the end of the day
When school is done.
We all run home
To our mum.

Jade Campion (9)
Bigyn CP School

ARTHUR

Arthur is my cat
he is black and fat.
His tail is long
but his legs are wrong.

Poor Arthur was born
one cold foggy morn.
Along with his twin
in the old garden bin.

His twin was called Sam
and he loved eating ham.
But Arthur, poor cat
his brain was all flat!

Although he's now old
he's still sleek and bold.
Arthur eats and he sleeps
But on his legs, only creeps.

Jack Hart (8)
Bigyn CP School

WALES

W indy weather when Wales play
A ll the time they win, hip, hip, hooray!
L lanelli we support you all the way
E njoy the match when they play
S ing and support them every day.

Chad White (9)
Bigyn CP School

SCARLETS

S carlets are the best, better than the rest,
C ardiff they can play, home or away.
A rms big and tough, the scores not enough,
R ugby shirts are dirty, the score is thirty
L lanelli always win, we'll stuff Neath in the bin,
E ars always taped up, Scarlets always hold the cup.
T racks from the skids, the crowds are full of kids
S orrow if they lose, but then drink the booze.

Liam Cole (9)
Bigyn CP School

St David's Day

S   ongs we sang
T   ales we told

D   id you hear about him?
A   good man he was
V   ery nice and good looking
I   would have loved to have met him.
D   id you know he was very kind?
S   aint David is his name.

D   ewi Sant in Welsh
A   Patron Saint of Wales
Y   ou will hear about him on March 1st.

Nicholas Davies (10)
Bigyn CP School

OUR HERO

The big day was arriving
The Cup Final was to be played
The sun was brightly shining,
And the trees gently swayed.
When we arrived at Stradey
Only red and blue jerseys could be seen.
Little children and their daddies
Others were adults and teens.
The whistle blew, and Cardiff kicked off,
Even birds looked as they flew.
At the match everyone had waited for
The game was pretty tight
We were behind 3 - 0 at half-time
Then Stephen Jones scored a try.
Oh what a lovely sight
We were in the dying minutes and
8 - 7 was the score
We all thought it was over
When the whistle blew once more.
But the ref gave us a pen, it was on the halfway line,
A kick for goal was our only option
It was almost full-time.
Stephen Jones placed the ball down
And the crowd screamed no more.
The kick was almost impossible
But it would change the score.
No one could look after his foot hit the ball,
But his face told the story, we had won after all.
So Stephen was our hero, on that great day,
Let's hope he can keep his great form
For the Cup Final in May.

Mark Davies (10)
Bigyn CP School

MY FRIEND SAM

My friend Sam
Doesn't care a bit,
If it's horrible or fine,
She says 'Let's keep fit!'
Or 'Let's make wine!'
We go swimming at the pool.
My friend Sam is so cool
Even though she is very tall.
She can never climb the wall
We go horse-riding together
Whatever the weather.
We like to cast funny spells
And throw coins down the well.
We also like to sing and dance
And skip around and jump and prance.
We like to dress up like pop stars,
We do not like boys and cars.
We watch my cat stalk its prey
On a sunny summer's day
Near or far
At peace or war,
She will always be my friend Sam!

Kayleigh Stevens (11)
Bigyn CP School

FRIENDS

Having friends is very nice, you
Can have a lot of fun have
A game of Rugby, or play around
In the sun.

You can sit and have a chat
or have a joking fight.

You can even if you like ask them
to stay the night.

Best of all my friend is a very special chum
her name is Mrs Thomas
I like to call her Mum.

Ashley Thomas (11)
Bigyn CP School

If I Was A Dragon

If I was a dragon I'd laze
around all day, just guarding
treasure in my cave.

When it comes to dinnertime
I'll blowtorch an animal.
If I had wings I'd fly around
all day and hope I don't hit
a tree, but the only problem
that I have now is I'm just
human me.

Christopher Daniel Smith (11)
Bigyn CP School

SCARLETS

S   carlets are the best
C   ome on Scarlets win the cup
A   fter all we are the best
R   ugby is the best thing
L   ets go beat the Jacks
E   normous crowds cheering
T   hem on come on
S   carlets here we come.

Jordan Sean Lucas (11)
Bigyn CP School

My Cat Topsey

My cat is crazy
My cat is lazy
She likes to play
The day away
She chases mice
She thinks they're nice and
A tasty bite.
She likes to watch birds
Fly in the sky and would
Like to eat them in a pie.
She lies in the sun
And seems to have fun
That's my cat Topsey.

Jamie Lee Morris (11)
Bigyn CP School

STARS

I know my stars
I know some more
I know some constellations
I've seen before

Up in the sky so bright
Twinkling like frost
Makes me feel so spacey
I could get lost

Call it what you like
Sol or sun
I know it's very hot
Our currant bun.

The winter's night sky
Is very cold indeed
But the stars that shine so brightly
I really love and need.

I love the moon
I love the stars
And I wouldn't mind
A trip to Mars.

Jamie Rogers (8)
Bigyn CP School

AUTUMN

In autumn the leaves turn red
And brown they are so pretty
I can't believe it
I wish I had a tree,
Oh boy, oh boy they're so nice
They're so nice.
Oh boy, oh boy!

Corey Jones (8)
Bigyn CP School

STONE COLD

I like to watch the wrestlers fight
Stone Cold grabs The Rock with all his might
He hits The Rock in the face so hard
He falls to the floor like a lump of lard

Stone Cold is the toughest one there
He's tougher than a grizzly bear
After the fight he has two cans of beer
Then he's so drunk, he's as weak as a deer

If I was a wrestler
I'd be the biggest one.
I'd hit them so hard
They'd fall on their bum.

Carl Jones (9)
Bigyn CP School

SPACE

I went to the library yesterday
and found a book about space.
I opened it and had a look at
the spiky sparkling stars.
I thought they were little diamonds
shooting past the moon.
I thought it was fun, the book about space.

I closed the book and imagined
me being an astronaut landing
in space.
I thought it would be fun
I took it to school and looked at it
all over again then I got sick
of reading the book about space.

Just then I had an idea
and shouted out.
'Space book for sale, only a pound'
Then at last a boy came up
and said 'I'll buy that space book
for three thousand pounds.'
'No thanks, I'll take a pound please!'

Carly Louise Dix (8)
Bigyn CP School

WEATHER

Rain, rain is a pain
To get wet all over again
When I go out
Without a coat
I'll find the sun
Come creeping out
Behind a cloud
One bright day
The sun will shine
Me on my way.

Jonathan Gordon
Bigyn CP School

COLOURS

There are lots of pretty colours
for you and me to see.
From the colours of the rainbow
to the colour of a tree.
From the darkness of the sky at night
to the brightness of morning light.
From the plants and flowers big and small
to all God's creatures one and all.
If I had to pick the colour that
I like the best.
I might say blue or red or green or
purple and yellow, they must be seen.

Pink and orange, black and white
all the colours are such a sight.

Colour is a wonderful thing
with all the joy they surely bring.

Jordan Elliott (8)
Bigyn CP School

VELCRO

V elcro is nice, very cute and friendly
E xtremely soft and furry, he plays all day and plays all night.
L oves to run and play in the day and night.
C an do lots of other things and hates to fight.
R uns up and down this big long pipe
O h he always eats his food in the morning and at night.

M y cat is always playful and bright
Y ou can see him and he will come to you

C an also jump up high because he is light
A nswers to his name on the first time
T hat's my cat Velcro, that's right.

Christian Williams (10)
Bigyn CP School

MY MATE FREDDY

My mate Freddy is so cool
He's even got his own swimming pool
He made a quick dash
And jumped with a splash
And drowned.
What a silly fool!

The ambulance came to rescue Freddy
It was too late,
He'd died already.

The day of the funeral, it was sunny and bright
Everything was a wonderful sight.
But poor old Freddy all bony and dead
Couldn't see anything, cos he didn't have a head.

Jamie Wilson (11)
Bigyn CP School

THE DYING STAR

I'm old
I'm cold
I'm going to die,
In a couple of weeks
I'm going red
I'm falling
My family
Are all young
But I'm not
My family are crying
I am too
It's a couple
Of days now
I'm afraid
I'm not
Very far now.
My family are
Staying up there
I'm not
My children
Want to come with me
I said 'No!'
One day now
I'm getting hot
I'm burning up
I'm really close now
My family are
Saying goodbye.
Bang!

Ben Lewis (10)
Bigyn CP School

FRIENDSHIP

F inding a good friend is
R eally hard and
I f you do, you are
E xtremely lucky.
N ever forget the good
D ays that you've
S pent together, during the
H olidays and even
I f you went shopping or
P erhaps to the swimming pool.

Sara Gibbons (10)
Bigyn CP School

STARS

Stars are
twinkling
awesome
really cool
sparkling like gems.

Interesting to look at in the night
twinkling planets
high in the sky
everywhere they

Shine
twinkly, sparkling stars for . . .
you to look at.

Leeanne Thomas (10)
Bigyn CP School

SOMEONE

Someone who will
laugh and joke
and if you're feeling down
give you a poke.
Someone who is
always there
and will always,
always share.
Give you sweets and
laugh a lot
and your birthday
never forgot
then you will never
ever end
for you have a special, special
friend!

Laura Jones (10)
Bigyn CP School

AMY

I have a dog named 'Amy'
She is very small
Even though I feed her
She won't grow very tall

Every day I walk her
Across the fields nearby
She plays and runs alongside me
But never runs away.

Sean Williams (10)
Bigyn CP School

SCAMPI

My hamster is so cute and small
He loves to scamper in his ball
He likes to eat his daily scone
One quick nibble and it's all gone
His fur is very soft and gold
He snuggles in his bed when cold
He looks at me oh so sweet
When I give him a chocolate treat
He loves to sit upon my lap
And often takes a little nap
But best of all he plays with me
My lovely hamster called Scampi.

Jennifer Brown (10)
Bigyn CP School

THE PRAYER

As I walked through a field so green
A wonderful sight which never before seen
Most divine in all its beauty
'Twas a vicar I spied doing his duty
On bended knees with hands together
Praying to God to give us fine weather
But alas his toil was all in vain
Just at that moment it poured down with rain
Up jumped the vicar in a terrible rage
But that's the end of the poem
Cos it's the end of the page.

Liam Jones (8)
Bigyn CP School

ONLY AFTER

Only after the last piece of
rubbish has been thrown,
Only after the last dolphin
has swum
Only after the last drop of oil
has been spilled
Only then will you find that you
can't repair the damage you
have made.

Emma Jade Jones (9)
Carwe Primary School

ONLY AFTER

Only after the last fox has been hunted
Only after the last oil spillage has happened
Only after the last animal is extinct
Only then will you find there will be no life.

Kieran Stephens (10)
Carwe Primary School

ONLY AFTER

Only after the last ocean has been filled with oil.
Only after the last bit of food has been eaten.
Only after the last school has been closed down.
Only then will you find that you can't be happy.

Joshua Andrews (10)
Carwe Primary School

ONLY AFTER

Only after the last dolphin has been caught
Only after the last child has been poisoned.
Only after the last lion has been shot
Only then will you find what you've lost.

Jessica Nicole Davies (8)
Carwe Primary School

MIDNIGHT VISITOR

A furry, fluffy cat
Moves slowly and quietly.
Soft cat
Nocturnal - hunts for food at night.

Christina Williams (8)
Carwe Primary School

MIDNIGHT VISITOR

Owl gliding through the air
hunting for food, doesn't care.
Sitting like a cat
looking for a rat.
His feathers look so nice
now he sees some little mice.

Samantha Lyons (8)
Carwe Primary School

MIDNIGHT VISITOR

Fox
Running as fast as an aeroplane
Sneaks out at night
Looking for food
Catches it to feed its cubs.

Curtis Elliott (8)
Carwe Primary School

MIDNIGHT VISITOR

Owls
in their furry coats
of brown and white.
Glide in the air
to catch their food.

Tia Mary Shelley Whiley (8)
Carwe Primary School

ONLY AFTER

Only after the last cow was killed
Only after the last rib has been eaten.
Only after the last bird has been shot
Only then will you realise that you
Can't bring lives back.

Daniel Michael Murphy (9)
Carwe Primary School

MIDNIGHT VISITOR

Cat
Sly through the grass
Sleeps all the time
Eats little mice
Purring, purring.

Ryan Morgan (7)
Carwe Primary School

MIDNIGHT VISITORS

Hedgehog comes snuffling
in the prickly grass.
Slowly he walks as soft as a mouse
scuffing the leaves for slugs and worms
in his prickly coat
until he sees a mouse.

Amy Oddy (7)
Carwe Primary School

ONLY AFTER

Only after the last dolphin has been poisoned
Only after the last gorilla has been shot
Only after the last child has been killed
Only then will you find that you cannot bring back
what you have lost.

Sarah Williams (9)
Carwe Primary School

ONLY AFTER

Only after the last dolphin has been killed
Only after the last school was closed down
Only after the last book was burned
Only then will you find that you
Cannot live without happiness.

Rebecca Mair Beynon (10)
Carwe Primary School

MIDNIGHT VISITOR

Fox.
Fox goes hunting at night
With orange coat
Going in the water
Fox jumps.

Jeremy Rees (8)
Carwe Primary School

ONLY AFTER

Only after the last cloud gives us rain
Only after the last field gives us food
Only after the last animal is killed
Only then will you find that pollution kills all.

Kyle Jones (8)
Carwe Primary School

ONLY AFTER

Only after the last rainfall
Only after the last happiness covers the world
Only after the last fish has been wasted
Only after the last sea has been destroyed by oil
Only then will you find that machines
and money aren't everything.

Richard Owens (11)
Carwe Primary School

WINTER COMES

So winter comes
We will have snow
And what will poor children do then, poor thing?
They'll go out in the snow
And do what they know
Then they come in all cold, poor thing.

As winter comes
We will have snow,
And what will poor snowman do then, poor thing?
He knows he'll get hit
Or pushed down a pit
But they don't care at all, poor thing.

Luke Helm (10)
Llangunnor CP School

THE ROBIN

Snow is here
Christmas cheer,
But not for poor Robin.

He'll head for a barn
Find some yarn,
And fluff up his feathers to keep warm.

Because of the snow
He has to keep low,
Safe in his nest in the roof.

Outside Jack Frost is at work,
Working on windows with a three-pronged fork
Everyone talks about Jack Frost at work.

Henry Young (10)
Llangunnor CP School

JACK FROST

Jack Frost has been over the town
Drawing on windows jumping around.

People do hate him for freezing their toes,
When the wind blows.

Trees standing there so bare,
Waiting for the summer to mend them with care.

Children playing on the ice,
With their mittens, warm and nice.

Mums and dads cooking the tea,
While little ones warm up their knees.

Animals and birds start to wake,
While the day begins to break.

Kathryn Marie Hughson (11)
Llangunnor CP School

A FISH CALLED FRANK

We have a fish his name is Frank
We keep him in a very big tank,
His colour is gold, red and white
He swims all day and rests all night.

Rhodri Jones (8)
Llangunnor CP School

SPRING POEM

Spring is lovely for little animals
Cats, birds and squirrels.
Cats miaow for food
The flowers smell lovely
The butterflies grow beautiful wings of patterns.

Kara Wray (8)
Llangunnor CP School

PLANETS

Pluto is the smallest planet
Light is from the sun which goes on the plants
And some planets are made out of water like
Neptune and Uranus
Earth is where we live.
We have towns in the sky
They don't.
Saturn has rings that are made out of rock.

Thomas Boucher (8)
Llangunnor CP School

SNAKES

Snakes
Snakes slither on the ground
Snakes hiss
Snakes slither
Softly on the ground
Snakes slither behind you . . .
You don't know where.
The snake is coming
To get you . . .
Oh no! It has got you!
Watch out!
You might be next!

Darcy Langdon (8)
Llangunnor CP School

SPRING

Spring brings sunshine
bees are busy buzzing around,
making yummy honey
for me and my mummy.
It definitely takes our minds off money!
Newborn lambs nibble the new spring grass.
Easter is coming, nobody is nasty, because
Mr Bunny is coming with chocolate eggs
for all the girls and boys; like Santa came to
most of us with lovely Christmas toys.
Newborn lambs are born today,
Hip, hip, *hooray* it's time to play!

Sophie Hill (8)
Llangunnor CP School

SNAKES

S nakes are slithery
N asty snakes spit poison
A ll snakes are vicious
K ing cobras spit deadly poison
E els look like snakes
S ometimes snakes whip people with their tails.

Daniel George (8)
Llangunnor CP School

THE OLD MAN FROM FRANCE

There was an old man from France
Who had ants in his pants
Even though he didn't know it
He was still able to show it
And wondered why he could dance.

Luke Totterdell (9)
Llangunnor CP School

MY BROTHER WILL

I love my brother Will
He's got beautiful golden hair
His eyes are blue like the sky
Well he's a boy
He likes to play with his favourite toys
Bikes, Lego and toy bricks
He's not snappy or cross
I love my brother Will.

Caroline James (8)
Llangunnor CP School

SPRING

S   is for sunflowers
P   is for petals on the flowers
R   is for roses smelling so sweet
I   is for inside looking out at the garden
N   is for flowers nodding and bobbing
G   is for growing - plants and flowers.

Matthew Granfield (9)
Llangunnor CP School

SPRING

When the sun fills the room
And the daffodils bloom
The days are getting longer
Plants are growing stronger
Frogs are spawning
Cockerels call in the morning
You hear the birds sing
And you know it is spring.

Ross McLennan (9)
Llangunnor CP School

SPRING

S   pring is a wonderful time
P   eaceful all the time
R   obins singing fine
I   n the barn the lambs are born
N   othing is loud
G   reat the plants are growing.

George Gleeson (9)
Llangunnor CP School

SPRING

S   pring is on its way
P   eople out to play
R   abbits hopping round
I   n the fields all day
N   o more ice and snow
G   lad it's gone away.

Christopher Thomas (8)
Llangunnor CP School

SPRING

S   pring is when everything is fresh
P   eople plant flowers
R   ain it does in spring
I   n spring people like going outside
N   o leaves are brown in spring
G   oing outside, people do in spring.

Daniel Ward (8)
Llangunnor CP School

SPRING

St David's Day marks the start of spring
The days are getting longer
The grass grows
Flowers start to sprout
Daffodils and tulips are everywhere
Lambs are running around the fields
And in the trees, birds build their nests.

Martyn Penhallurick (8)
Llangunnor CP School

SPRING

In the spring the sun comes out
Lots of lambs go jumping about
Leaves come back onto the trees
Then we see some bumblebees
Daffodils grow, primroses, snowdrops too
Smiling happily up at you.

Sam Davies (9)
Llangunnor CP School

SCHOOL

Ring, ring the bell goes
Countless walk through the corridor into class
Learning, learning that's all we do
Some get maths wrong, they say 'Doh!'
Some get it right, they say 'Yes!'
Children ask silly questions
Some say remember the rules
Ring, ring the dinner bell goes
In we go to get food.
Please and thank you we said for food
Next lesson in we go.

Rhodri Evans (11)
Llanybydder Primary School

A WALK IN THE PARK

Springtime walking in the park,
the stones rustling under your feet.
Trees full of leaves.
But wait! An apple, a
golden apple in a tree,
but it is totally protected,
no branches to climb
too high to jump.
How do you get there?
How? No one knows.

Oliver Florence (11)
Llanybydder Primary School

WAR IS WRONG

The war has begun
Heroic warriors fight
Extreme force is used

War is in mid stage
A life is lost every second
Right! War is not.

It should be locked up and never released
So is this our main aim, if it is
War should be practised. No way!
Wrong to murder, sad is death
On this day I declare it banished
No! Is that what you'd say
Go on then, wipe us out.

Paul Bashford (11)
Llanybydder Primary School

THE CAT

The cat sits by the fire all day
She chases mice in March and May.
She does not care about the dogs
But she does care about the frogs.

She is a very strange cat
Because she plays with a bat.
When she tries to catch the mice
She only fails once or twice.

Lowri Haf Davies (10)
Llanybydder Primary School

THE PLANETS

Swerving around in space
Floating in the air
All around there's darkness
With its colourful glare.

Scientists try to discover
What a planet really is
Studying day and night
When they look in a telescope,
There's no star in sight.

Spacemen; men going into space
With an oxygen helmet on their face,
Seeing wonderful things around
Soon the planets will be found

Neil Armstrong was very brave
Walking on the moon,
I think someone else will go into space
And let's hope it's very soon.

Shaun Ablett (11)
Llanybydder Primary School

A HORSE'S LIFE

The horses galloping in competitions
The hounds and the men
Chasing foxes
The horse is chewing grass
All day long
Sleeping in the sun

The brown eyes
His big ears
His enormous mouth to eat
His legs for jumping high, over the fences,
His tail for beauty
His tongue for the taste of grass
The herd of horses in the sun.

Jonathan Davies (11)
Llanybydder Primary School

UNDER THE SEA

Deep, deep under the sea
Fishes to meet you and me
Sharks and dolphins
Starfish even
Sea horses swim
Like the pink octopus Kim
Can't forget the jellyfish no
Carry on swimming deep deep down
See what you can see
I've named mine.

Jade Jones (10)
Llanybydder Primary School

THE DEEP

In the sea, deep, deep down
See the fishes flapping around.
People swimming up above
Like a duck or a swan.
Octopuses, dolphins, sharks are swimming.
People are fishing
Sharks are chasing
Dolphins are swimming
Fishes are flapping
Jellyfishes are stinging
Watch out for them.

Alison Lucas (11)
Llanybydder Primary School

LIVING ON THE STREETS

No food, no drink
life stinks
Nothing to do
I have no clue
What to do today

I wish I was rich
Like that guy Mich
Because he's so rich

I sleep in a box
It has no locks
I don't have Christmas presents
And my Christmas dinner
Is only a packet of chicken crisps
If I'm lucky

So I have told
you my life and it
stinks!

David Anthony Jones (11)
Llanybydder Primary School

BALLS

Big balls,
      Small balls,
Shiny balls
      Glitter balls
See-through balls
      3D balls
What a lot of balls there are
      I hope I get a ball some day.

Gareth Jones (10)
Llechryd School

WAR

Bombs bombing all around,
knives stuck in the ground,
blood pouring from bodies.
British and German men
fighting like Rottweiler dogs.

Women and children screaming
to see such a place,
not many homes still standing.
What a disgrace.

Children clinging to their families
in despair
planes dropping bombs through
the air.

Men crying for help,
but there is no help.

After the war
children play
and look away

From their fathers' and grandfathers' photographs.

Kelly Morrisey (10)
Llechryd School

COLOURS OF THE UNIVERSE

Rapid mercury, hidden by the sun's light
Hot Venus, brown with golden tiger stripes,
Mars, a harsh red desert
Jupiter, the banded red and orange giant
With a storm the size of Earth.
Yellowy ringed Saturn is next
The cold blue Uranus
Neptune too is blue
And tiny Pluto has a brownish hue
Earth, our beloved planet
Has water, all so blue
Yellow, brown and green land
With animals, people and you!

Rebecca Sommerville (10)
Llechryd School

GRAVITY

Gravity keeps you down
Keeps you standing
On the ground
Gravity
       Gravity
              Grav-it-y

Gravity stops me jumping
Jumping up so high
Gravity stops me jumping
Jumping to the sky.
Gravity
       Gravity
              Grav-it-y.

Wyn Jones (8)
Llechryd School

THE KING

The king was a very strange man
He put his dog in a frying pan

When it was time for his supper
He ate a ton of buffalo butter

When it was time for his tea
He went down to the red sea.

Then he went in his leaky boat
Around the castle's reeking moat.

Francis Barrett (10)
Llechryd School

THE MOON AND STARS

Glittery moon
Glittery stars
I am in your light

Glittery moon
Glittery stars
You come out at night

Glittery moon
Glittery stars
What a lovely sight.

Hannah Curran (8)
Llechryd School

MARS

Mars is red and fiery
When you look at it in a book
It makes you feel scared
No wonder the Romans
Named it after the God of War

        Campaigns
        Combat
        Crusades
        Fighting
        Hostilities
        Military Action
        Warfare -
All to do with Mars
Fiery red planet, the colour of blood.

Antoni Castaglioni (10)
Llechryd School

MY FAMILY

My brother's name is Chris
He's so very, very cool
He loves drawing animals
O yappy, yappy do.

My sister's name is Kat
She's so very, very cool
She loves making things
O yappy, yappy do.

My mum's name is Helen
She's so very, very cool
She loves planting things
O yappy, yappy do.

My dad's name is John
He's so very, very cool
He likes fixing things
O yappy, yappy do.

And my name is Kerry
I'm so very, very cool
I love writing poems
O yappy, yappy do.

Kerry Thomas (9)
Llechryd School

ROME WAS A BEAUTIFUL HOME

Rome was a beautiful home
Much better than the Millennium Dome
When the Romans planned an attack
They hit the enemy with a Centurion pack
And built roads as straight as can be
That's why they went down in history.

Aled James (9)
Llechryd School

BOOKS

Magical
Mysterious
Adventurous
Spine-tickling
Fantastic
Factual
Poetic
Informative
I love books.

John Williams (9)
Llechryd School

ALED IN SPACE

Aled James, he goes to space
In his bright red rocket
He wants to visit planet Mars
And then of course, the shining stars.

He's ready with his sandwiches
He's ready with his pack
Aled James, he goes to space
And then he comes right back.

Adrian Hutton (9)
Llechryd School

FRIENDS

What are friends for?
> Playing with
> Working with
> Having fun with
> Laughing with

> They are company
> When you are sad
> They are company
> When you are glad

> Sharing secrets
> Playing games
> Dressing up
> Singing songs

> They are company
> When you are sad
> They are company
> When you are glad

That's what friends are for.

Ruth Sommerville (9)
Llechryd School

MY DOG

My dog Lucky
Loves her food
My dog Lucky
Loves being stroked
My dog Lucky
Plays with me
My dog Lucky
Is my friend
      - Playful
      - Happy
      - Funny
      - Scruffy
      - Fabulous
My dog Lucky.

Bethan Curran (9)
Llechryd School

SCHOOL

I love school,
It's so very, very cool.
School is great,
Lots of mates.
Maths is maths,
I'm sitting in the class.
Here I am, here I am
Here I am.

Angharad Rees (8)
Llechryd School

SPACE

One night
    I flew into space
    In my super rocket
    Flying through the air
    Without any care
    Aiming for the stars.

Megan Williams (8)
Llechryd School

THE LONELY CHILD

I stand alone in the playground
I stand and watch the day go round
I stand and wait to be picked
As they choose their team for the cricket pitch.
I stand and watch the children play
I wait for the bell at the end of the day.

Kayley Gebbie (11)
Nant-Y-Groes Primary School

MY FAMILY

My name is Anna-Jayne
and I am sometimes a pain.
I am ten years old and I have a cold.
My favourite colour is red
and I like to snuggle up in bed.

My brother's name is Matthew Davies
his favourite colour is green, he is very, very mean.
His room is full of food and he is very rude.
He likes to eat meat, but he does not like to eat wheat.

My mother's name is Melanie Davies
she is nice but sometimes I want to boil her like rice.
My mum gets mad when I take her money
then other times she is very funny.

My father's name is Keith and he has big, yellow teeth.
My dad likes planes which is a pain
because he wants to fly to Spain.

Anna Davies (10)
Nant-Y-Groes Primary School

My Brothers

My brother Darren is very mean his favourite colour is green.
He likes his food and likes to eat. He also has smelly feet.
He's like a giant, he's really tall, unlucky for me I'm really small.
He likes his football and is very good,
he could be a pro, I wish he would.
He makes me laugh because he's very funny
but makes me cry when I take his money.
My brother Carl has lots of hair, he's very strong, he broke my chair.
His favourite football team is Aston Villa,
he likes ice-cream especially vanilla.
His favourite colour is blue, he wants to be a farmer - that is true
he likes to colour and play with me, no he doesn't, he's too lazy.
He's got a car and is very kind,
he takes me up my Gran's, he doesn't mind.
I like my brothers they're not that bad after all the fun we have.
Come to think that is wrong, they've bullied me for far too long
they don't hurt me or injure me, I can tell that they love me.
One more thing I forgot to mention
that has just been brought to my attention
my brothers are not that bad, although they can make me quite mad.

Leanne Jones (9)
Nant-Y-Groes Primary School

SUMMER

S   wimming under the water is nice and cool.
U   mbrellas are nice and shady.
M   um covers me in a coat of sun cream.
M   aking sandcastles which fall down in the water.
E   arly in the morning we go to the beach.
R   ocks in the rock pool reflect the sunshine.

Samantha Griffiths (8)
Old Road Primary School

SPRING

S   howers pouring down from the sky
P   retty flowers grow from the ground
R   eturning home, here come the birds
I   n the house I run safe from the rain
N   ew lambs are born in springtime
G   row pretty flowers, grow.

Lloyd Davies (8)
Old Road Primary School

AUTUMN SEASON

A   corns fall from the sky
U   nder the woodland trees
T   rees scaley, tall and strong
U   nder our feet lay a blanket of leaves
M ist covers the darkness
N   estling creatures settle for the night.

Joshua Naylor (7)
Old Road Primary School

WINTER

W inter snow is on the ground
I   ce makes you fall
N ight gets darker sooner
T rees covered in snow stand tall
E verywhere is crisp and cold
R eal snow is all around.

Peter Harris (8)
Old Road Primary School

1 To 10

One wavy waterlogged waterfall
Two tall teachers talking
Three tiny teeth tickling
Four fantastic friends fighting
Five fish fighting
Six silent snakes slithering
Seven stars sparkling
Eight Easter eggs
Nine naughty nephews
Ten terrified teachers.

Rebecca Wilkins (10)
Old Road Primary School

OAKWOOD PARK

Asked to Oakwood Park
Bet Ben would go on Vertigo
Couldn't find my way to the Toboggan
Dripping wet with water
Exciting rides on Megaphobia
Fabulous French fries freshly cooked
Giant towers for a water ride
Horrible skulls in the Haunted House
Impossible drops on Bounce
Jet fast rollercoaster fling round and round
Kebabs sizzling
Lovely barbecue at the end of the night.

Timothy Taylor (10)
Old Road Primary School

RABBITS

Rare and cute
Omnivore
Soft, harmless
Giving warmness in the heart when stroked and fed
Playing but watching for foxes
Hoping their family will go on.

Hayley Evans (9)
Old Road Primary School

ICE

Gleams, slips
Smooth, cold, hard
Transparent,
Cold-hearted,
Fun but dangerous.

Kate Davies (9)
Old Road Primary School

FLIES

Tiny and quick
Careful about being caught
Horrible and disgusting
Not the sort of pet you
Would want to have.

Rebecca Crabb (9)
Old Road Primary School

WHEN WILL I . . .

When will I grow up?
I will never stop.
What makes us what we are?
We make us what we are.
What is silence?
Silence is a dream or a whisper.
Where do echoes go?
Echoes fade away slowly up to Heaven.
Where is the end of the rainbow?

Sophia Williams (9)
Old Road Primary School

TOWN

All went to town
Great sales were on
Bought a lot of clothes
Called in the shops
Dicksons was closed
Friends passed by
Rushing to the shops
Idea to buy a pet
Jogged to the pet shop
But loving all the toys
Killer prices!

Jamie Mends (10)
Old Road Primary School

THE SUN

Shines, glitters, sparkles
Hot, sharp, spiky
Gold, yellow, orange and lemon
Filling the sky with brightness
Burning on my skin
Peppery, chillies and hot and spicy
Look I'm burnt!

Carolyn Gemma Rees (10)
Old Road Primary School

I'D LIKE TO BE . . .

Where does the universe begin?
In God's hands.
What are colours for?
For brightness in the world.
Why do we learn?
To teach one another.
What is death?
When our life is over.
What are we designed for?
To keep the world clean.

Simon Lewis (10)
Old Road Primary School

THE UNUSUAL CLASS

There was an unusual class
Who were a very big mess
They hardly knew anything
Except for the bell that went ding

There was a boy called Jake
Who once wrestled a snake
His mum was baking a cake
When he fell in the lake

He then
Ate a pea
And drowned a flea
His spilt his tea
Then he met a lovely lady

There was a girl called Daisy
Who was very lazy
She was a terrible athlete
She ate a lot of meat
Then she met a boy called Pete

There was a boy called Pete
Who had really smelly feet
He had a little meat
And sat on a very wet seat

There was a girl called Nicola
Who drunk a lot of cola
She really loved koalas
Actually she acts like one

There was a boy called Jack
Who always wears a Mac
And always wears a hat

This is all about the class
Who made a very big mess
Finally they got better
But not that much!

Michelle Crabb (10)
Old Road Primary School

I HATE SCHOOL
(In the tune of Jingle Bells)

Oh I hate school
I hate school, ho . . . ho . . . homework too
It's hard and boring
It's just like snoring
My maths book tells me so

Oh I hate Welsh
I hate science
PE is so fun!
Art's creative and imaginative
That's what I live for!

Lorna Gravelle (11)
Old Road Primary School

FOOTSTEPS ON MY PATH

Footsteps on my snowy path,
as white as white can be.
I turned around to look
and guess what I could see?
Elephants walking up my street,
plid-plod, plid-plod.
Elephants walking up my path,
plid plod, plid plod.
I sat down on my doorstep to think what to do,
then I remembered about the zoo.
Two elephants had escaped from the zoo that day,
so I rode them back and there they had to stay.
So when I am walking up my snowy path
I think of elephants and start to laugh and laugh!

Charlotte Rose Williams (11)
Old Road Primary School

AUTUMN

A corns fall off the trees
U nusual colours
T rees hide the sleeping animals
U nder the cover of darkness
M ighty colourful leaves
N ights get longer.

Jamie Baier (7)
Old Road Primary School

WINTER

W inter snow falls heavily
I   ce is very, very slippery
N ights are getting darker
T rees are very beautiful
E mergency on the roads
R obins come out in the winter.

James Southam (8)
Old Road Primary School

SUMMER

S   un is warm
U   mbrella saves me from the sun
M um covers me in a cloak of suncream
M ustn't paddle too far out
E   nd of the day is here
R   eturn home from a lazy summer's day.

Ffion Richards (8)
Old Road Primary School

ICE

Cold and slippery
Smooth but hard
Transparent and silver
Slippery and slidy
Fun but dangerous.

Daniel Mark Griffiths (9)
Old Road Primary School

TOWNS

Towns
Smelly, crowded
Hard and rough, difficult to touch
Unlikeable, lonely without friends
There must be a better place?

Chris Williams (9)
Old Road Primary School

HOLIDAYS

Packing suitcases with excitement
Driving off in the car
Staying in a posh hotel
Or camping out of doors
Holidays!

Stephen Lott (8)
Old Road Primary School

HOLIDAYS

Visiting friends and family
School quietly empty
Swimming in the Leisure Centre every day
Playing out in the sunshine with friends
Holidays.

Simon Walters (9)
Old Road Primary School

MY MUM

Shouting very loudly,
Cooking lovely meals for the family
Always working extra hard
Kissing me at bedtime
My mum!

James Lloyd (9)
Old Road Primary School

SPRING

Yellow buttercups shining brightly,
Sweet chocolate Easter eggs melted,
Large pancakes made yet again unsuccessfully,
Fresh birds returning and singing sweetly
    Spring!

Kimry Coleman (8)
Old Road Primary School

HOLIDAYS

Visiting friends every day
Splashing very noisily
Playing 'Mob' quietly
Watching television lazily
Holidays!

Alex Wilkins (8)
Old Road Primary School

SPRING

Lambs playing noisily
Children shouting noisily
Birds tweeting gently
Flowers growing prettily
Spring!

Andrew Jackson (9)
Old Road Primary School

My Mum

Kissing me every day
Shopping with the family
Voice thundering loudly
Cooking delicious meals
My mum!

Shaun Caton (9)
Old Road Primary School

My Mum

Giving me a kiss before I go to bed
Cleaning upstairs and downstairs
Shopping in Asda for food
Cooking meals for me, Dad and herself
My mum!

Daniel James (9)
Old Road Primary School

THE PITY OF LOVE

A pity beyond all telling
Is hid in the heart of love
The folk who are buying and selling
The clouds on their journey above
The cold, wet winds ever blowing and the shadowy haze
Where waters are flowing
Threaten the head that I love.

Laura Thomas (9)
Swiss Valley Primary School

ANIMALS

Animals rule the world!
Since the snake curled
Since the worm squirmed
They have ruled!

Sea animals rule the ocean!
You must use caution
Don't you just love the whale's motion?

Land animals rule the land!
The camels stroll on the hot desert sand
The tigers run after the antelope band!

Tree animals rule the trees!
These animals are up high,
Be careful they don't bring you to your knees!

Sally Davies (9)
Swiss Valley Primary School

IS IT A DREAM?

When I woke that stormy night,
I rode upon a horse so bright,
The night my track,
My voice was lost,
Is it a dream?

I shook off sleep as it came again,
Its form now that of an eagle great,
Its glossy feathers; its beating wings,
Its sleek head; its sharpened claws,
Is it a dream?

This night to me as a fox it came,
A hunting, elegant, golden fox,
It pattered up to my desolate room,
It roused me from my slumber,
Is it a dream?

Is it a dream when I lie back still,
Listening to the cruel wolves howl?
Is it a dream when I wake at night,
An outside noise that woke me?
Is life a dream?

Nikita Poli (9)
Swiss Valley Primary School

CAN I HAVE...

Can I have a chocolate bar?
Later darling, I'm going to the Spar.
Can I have a new toy?
Not now, I'm going to see my friend's baby boy.
Can I have your bedroom?
Now, where's that garden broom?
Can I have a new computer,
Or maybe a new scooter?

Can I have a teddy?
I'm going out, I have to get ready!
Can I have a new CD?
Wait a minute, your father needs me.
Can I have a lollipop?
This nagging has just got to stop!
Look mammy it's Aunty Lyn.
Shut up! You're doing my head in!

Lauren Sourbutts (9)
Swiss Valley Primary School

GREAT GRUB

Stop! Wait! Hold on a tick,
All those sweets will make you sick.
Think! Pause! Are you eating what you oughta?
Lots of fruit and vegetables, washed down with ice-cold water.
Crisps! Sweets! Rotting your teeth away,
Think about your smile and what your friends will say.
Pop! Cakes! Enough to sink a ship,
Think twice before eating another greasy chip.
Colourful! Crispy food that's healthy is not as boring as you think,
Pasta Carbonara and fresh squeezed juice to drink.
Refreshing! Tasty! A great way to stop you yawning,
Fresh cold milk and cereal starting off your morning,
Crunchy! Juicy! Fruit of all colours that shops sell,
But best of all's the energy you feel when you eat well.
Stop! Think! You are what you eat,
It's not about not eating all the things you call a treat.
Think! Pause! A balanced diet's the only way,
It's not about depriving yourself forever and a day.

Hannah Morris (9)
Swiss Valley Primary School

IF I HAD MY WAY

I'm a nine year old girl in a class,
Of a school which, if I had my way
Would be a place where children went
To sing and dance and play.

I'm a nine year old girl eating food
Which if I had my way,
Would not be broccoli, carrots and peas,
But sweeties every day!

I'm a nine year old girl in a country
Which if I had my way,
Would only rain on certain nights
And the sun would shine all day!

I'd give my opinion in public,
But from this poem you can plainly see,
I'm only nine years older than a baby!
So who's going to listen to me?

Arianwen Caiach-Taylor (9)
Swiss Valley Primary School

BABBLEBOOTS

Babbleboots my cat,
Wears a funny hat.
The hat is red and blue,
With a bit of yellow too.
The hat is like a crate,
On top there's a plate.
On the plate there's chips,
And a pair of big fat lips.
The lips are juicy red,
And they're waiting to be fed.
I feed them every day,
With marmalade and hay.
He loves his little hat,
Does Babbleboots my cat.

Ffion L Halfpenny (10)
Ysgol Gynradd Cwmgors

MY DOG

My dog is always chewing on a log,
playing about as we go out,
and then goes to play
with the other dog, Mog.

My dog doesn't want to play,
she sits there all day.
As we stare at her,
looking at her wonderful fur.
Then off to bed after she is fed.

My dog is up and running,
and she's just playing.
No stop for food,
she's in a very good mood.
I wish this day could last,
it is going very fast.

Sarah Symons (10)
Ysgol Gynradd Cwmgors

WORLD WAR II

Bombs are coming,
Troops are running.
Children are playing,
Parents are praying.
Flashes of light,
In the night,
Giving everybody a fright,
Waiting for broad daylight.
Morning has broke in the smoke.
Sirens have stopped,
Planes have dropped.
People are dying,
Children are crying
And babies are born at dawn.

Martin Reddy (10)
Ysgol Gynradd Cwmgors

FLOWERS

F   is for floppy when they sit in the garden
L   is for lovely, how pretty they are
O   is for orchids, everybody likes them
W   is for wavy when they blow in the wind
E   is for enormous bunch of flowers
R   is for roses so appealing and nice
S   is for sunflower, so big and pleasing.

Kimberley Lewis (11)
Ysgol Gynradd Cwmgors

TRIP TO DISNEYLAND

The rides were thrilling
Roundabouts are spinning
In the haunted house
Phantoms and ghosts are chilling.

The parades were colourful and bright
Oh, what a beautiful sight.

Donald Duck quacking around
I hate that awful sound.
Singing and dancing on the street
No one stood still, they all tapped their feet.
Everyone cheered as the parade went by,
You could see Peter Pan up in the sky.
Lines of characters like Pluto and Goofy
All of them are very lovely.
Never before have I seen such a thing
'Daddy!' I shout, 'Can I go again?'

Nia Morris (10)
Ysgol Gynradd Cwmgors

JOURNEY THROUGH LONDON

P reparing for our journey ahead
O nly an hour to be bored in the head
E veryone bringing their travelling games
T ill the fumes go to our brains
I nto the London traffic we go
C ars, vans and buses travelling so slow

V ery stressed people beeping and tooting
O nly the ones that have to go to a meeting
Y achts are racing down the Thames
A fter a while we pass Big Ben
G iggling and laughing when we got there
E veryone running to see Aunty Claire
S taying the night to see London's Mayor.

Steffan Davies (11)
Ysgol Gynradd Cwmgors

MY PET JESS

I have a pet called Jess
I know he is truly the best
He never makes a mess
And that's my pet Jess

His colour is black and white
His eyes are so bright
Sometimes in the night
He gives me a fright.

Cerith Williams (10)
Ysgol Gynradd Cwmgors

MY PET

I have a dog called Cassie
And she can't see very well
She wags her tail every day
Until the sun goes down
She lies on the mat snoring
Twitching herself around
Thinking of all the rabbits
Hopping along the ground
Her legs and ears keep moving
You can see she's sniffing around
And on her magic dream she goes
Playing ball or with another hound
She used to be very lively
But now she's very old
She can't do things she used to do
Except lie there and snore
I don't think that's all she does
I think that she has lots of fun
Travelling around in her dreams
But at the end of the day
After all her dreams
She's always at home for me.

Gareth Thomas (11)
Ysgol Gynradd Cwmgors

IT'S A PIRATE'S LIFE FOR ME

It's a pirate's life for me.
Yo, ho, ho and a bottle of rum.
I get sea sick on the sea.
Yo, ho, ho and a bottle of rum.
Let's go sailing on the sea.
Yo, ho, ho and a bottle of rum.
Ahoy, ahoy a hoist that flag just for me.
Yo, ho, ho and a bottle of rum.
Smuggling rum and whisky.
Yo, ho, ho and a bottle of rum.
Joshua would like to be a sailor to sail the big blue sea.
Yo, ho, ho and a bottle of rum.
We'll even put a patch on his eye.
Treasure is the thing for me.
Yo, ho, ho and a bottle of rum.
Mr Edwards teaches me.
Yo, ho, ho and a bottle of rum.

Joshua Jones (10)
Ysgol Gynradd Cwmgors

AUTUMN

Animals playing in the brown crusty leaves,
Umbrellas blowing in the breeze,
Tortoises hibernating in their shells,
Squirrels collecting nuts,
People stamping on brown leaves,
Children splashing in puddles,
People wearing hat and scarves,
Flowers die off ready to shoot up next spring.

Bobbie Jones (10)
Ysgol Gynradd Cwmgors